Searchlight BOOKS™

Getting into Government

Exploring the Legislative Branch

Danielle Smith-Llera

Lerner Publications ◆ Minneapolis

Lerner Publications Company
A division of Lerner Publishing Group, Inc.
241 First Avenue North
Minneapolis, MN 55401 USA

For reading levels and more information, look up this title
at www.lernerbooks.com.

Library of Congress Cataloging-in-Publication Data

Names: Smith-Llera, Danielle, 1971– author.
Title: Exploring the legislative branch / Danielle Smith-Llera.
Description: Minneapolis : Lerner Publications, [2020] | Series: Searchlight books.
    Getting into government | Audience: Ages: 8–11. | Audience: Grades: 4 to 6. | Includes
    bibliographical references and index.
Identifiers: LCCN 2018057825 (print) | LCCN 2019005146
    (ebook) | ISBN 9781541556775 (eb pdf) | ISBN 9781541555877 (lib. bdg. : alk. paper) |
    ISBN 9781541574809 (pbk. : alk. paper)
Subjects: LCSH: United States. Congress—Juvenile literature. | United States.
    Congress—Powers and duties—Juvenile literature. | Legislation—United States—
    Juvenile literature. | United States—Politics and government—Juvenile literature.
Classification: LCC JK1025 (ebook) | LCC JK1025 .S55 2020 (print) | DDC 328.73—dc23

LC record available at https://lccn.loc.gov/2018057825

Manufactured in the United States of America
1-46042-43365-3/5/2019

Contents

Chapter 1

DUTIES OF THE LEGISLATIVE BRANCH

Bang! A gavel strikes a desk in the US Capitol in Washington, DC. Silence falls across the room holding the 435 men and women of the House of Representatives. On the other side of the building, a gavel also brings meetings of the 100-member Senate to order. Both groups make up the US Congress. Together, they share the important job of making laws for the nation.

To get the day started, the Speaker of the House bangs the gavel on the desk. This tells the 435 members of the House of Representatives that it's time to get to work.

Members of the House of Representatives welcome the new Speaker.

Inside the Capitol

Visitors watch from balconies inside both chambers. At first, the work of the legislature can seem quiet. Congress members shuffle papers and huddle to speak privately. But sometimes members rise to debate, and excitement can fill the room during a vote. Members call out yea or nay from their seats. This is what democracy looks like.

Behind the Constitution

In the late eighteenth century, Americans fought a war against Great Britain to elect a Congress like this. Before the Revolutionary War (1775–1783), American

colonists could not send representatives to vote on laws made in Parliament, Britain's governing body. But they still had to obey Britain's laws. This experience was on the minds of the authors of the US Constitution in 1787.

In the eighteenth century, American colonists were ruled by the British.

The Constitution set up rules for the US government, laws, and basic rights for all Americans.

When they wrote the Constitution, the authors mentioned the powers of Congress first—ahead of those of the executive branch and the judicial branch. The Constitution even gave Congress the power to approve Supreme Court justices and the president's advisers.

Voting Power

Voters elect members of the House of Representatives and Senate. These members of Congress work in Washington, DC, and make laws that affect the lives of everyone in the nation. That's why voters must carefully consider the ideas and leadership skills of the people they elect.

Members of Congress must be US citizens and live in the state they represent. Representatives must be at least twenty-five years old, and senators must be at least thirty.

Voters also elect members to their state legislatures. They make laws that affect the citizens of that state.

When Alexandria Ocasio-Cortez took office in January 2019, she became the youngest woman ever to serve in the US House of Representatives. She was twenty-nine years old.

That's a Fact!

The Constitution gives Congress the power to declare war. In 1812, members of Congress voted to go to war with Great Britain again. They never imagined that their workplace would burn to ruins during this war. British soldiers invaded Washington, DC, and set the Capitol on fire. After the war, the Capitol Building was rebuilt with a dome made of copper. It was updated again in the 1850s and made of fireproof cast iron.

During the War of 1812, the British burned many US government buildings, including the Capitol and the White House.

Chapter 2

AN INSIDE LOOK AT CONGRESS

Having two branches of Congress helped solve a problem for the leaders writing the Constitution. State leaders worried about how much power they would have in Congress. States with many residents thought they should be allowed to send more people to Congress. But smaller states with fewer residents wanted an equal voice in Congress.

Oliver Ellsworth (*left*) and Roger Sherman came up with the Connecticut Compromise—a plan that pleased states of different sizes.

This map shows the number of representatives that each state sends to the US House of Representatives.

Sharing Power

Having both a House of Representatives and a Senate pleased states of every population size. In the Senate, all states have equal power because each state elects two senators. Meanwhile, the population of each state determines how many representatives each state sends to the House. California, for example, has fifty-three representatives, while Wyoming has only one.

A raised platform in each chamber holds a desk for a leader. The Speaker of the House sits there with a US flag draped behind the desk. A blue-and-gold curtain hangs behind the Senate's most important desk. The vice president of the United States has a role in the Senate. But his only duty is to vote if there is a tie on an issue.

The Speaker of the House sits at the front of the room.

IN BOTH THE HOUSE AND SENATE, DEMOCRATS SIT ON ONE SIDE OF THE ROOM AND REPUBLICANS SIT ON THE OTHER.

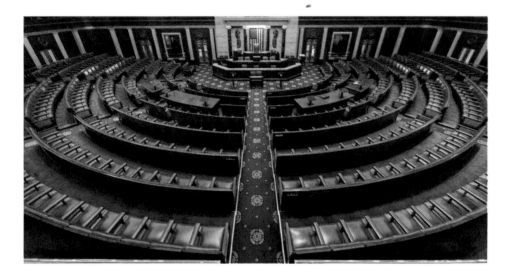

Do you like to sit near your friends in class? Congress members like to sit with the same group every day too. In the House of Representatives, members of the Democratic Party fill the seats on the Speaker's right. Members of the Republican Party sit on the left. The desks in the Senate are organized in the same way. Aisles run down each chamber separating these groups.

Different Views

Different ideas about the role of the government also divide these two groups. Democrats tend to believe the government should control the power of businesses and spend money to help citizens in need. Republicans tend to want a smaller federal government with fewer rules and regulations. Most arguments during debates in Congress occur between members across the center aisle.

Sometimes members from both the House and Senate come together. Here, they have gathered to hear the president speak.

Government Affects You

States and towns once passed unfair laws that forced black people and white people to live separately. They could not sit together in movie theaters, in restaurants, or on buses. Black people and white supporters protested to show the nation's leaders that this was unacceptable. They marched through cities and sat down together in public places. Police often arrested them. Congress finally passed a federal law in 1964 that made these unfair state laws illegal.

In the 1960s, civil rights supporters worked hard to get Congress to change unfair laws.

Chapter 3

MAKING LAWS

The Capitol's dome rises between the House of Representatives and the Senate chambers. Formal ceremonies take place in the vast, round room below—but not the messy work of making laws.

The House of Representatives is located in the south wing of the Capitol. The Senate occupies the north wing.

Sharing Duties

Both branches of Congress divide the work of making laws and important decisions. For example, all bills to raise money for the federal government must start in the House of Representatives. These bills become laws that tell citizens how much to pay in federal taxes. Meanwhile, only the Senate can approve treaties with other countries that the president suggested.

The Tax Cuts and Jobs Act bill was made into a law in 2017.

TAX CUTS AND JOBS ACT

From Idea to Bill to Law

Both chambers work together to pass laws. US citizens can send ideas for new laws to the representatives or senators from their state. When an idea starts in the House, representatives discuss it with one another. If enough representatives support the idea, it is written down and called a bill. The same happens in the Senate.

In the House of Representatives, bills are placed in the hopper.

In the House of Representatives, bills are placed in a wooden box called a hopper. Each bill is given a number, and the journey begins. First, members of the House discuss whether it should be passed. The Speaker of the House chooses a group of representatives to form a committee and review the bill. Each member of these committees is an expert on a topic, such as agriculture, education, or health.

House committee members discuss a bill in December 2017.

Committee members study the bill, research the topic, and may even make changes to it. Then they present the bill to all members of the House and vote. If a majority of representatives do not favor the bill, it fails. It has no chance of becoming a law. Most bills never survive this vote.

A Few Winners

Successful bills face both chambers of Congress. For example, if most representatives favor a bill, it travels to the Senate for approval. There, it passes through more committees, debates, and votes. If most senators vote for the bill, it heads to the White House. There, the president can sign the bill to make it a law. Or the president can veto, or reject, it. But the bill can still become law if two-thirds of all representatives and senators support it in a new vote. If the president ignores the bill, it can still become law. If ten days pass and Congress is in session, the bill becomes a law.

President Lyndon Johnson signs a bill into law.

Thousands of bills are introduced during each two-year session of Congress. Yet only about 5 to 10 percent become laws. Only the most popular bills become laws. But members of Congress can still introduce bills to adjust these laws. The US Supreme Court can also strike down a law if it doesn't follow the Constitution.

Members of the US Supreme Court, the highest court in the United States

That's a Fact!

A senator once spoke in the Senate for more than twenty-four hours without stopping! This dramatic way to delay or stop the passage of a bill is called a filibuster. Another filibuster involved members of Congress who believed that federal laws should not control how states handle equal rights. They organized a filibuster that lasted sixty days! To fill the time during a filibuster, speakers have sometimes read from Shakespeare and given recipes.

Senator Strom Thurmond holds the record for the longest filibuster in US history. He spoke against the Civil Rights Act of 1957 for more than twenty-four hours straight.

Chapter 4

THE LEGISLATIVE BRANCH AND YOU

Congress members must consider what interests their voters. Voters in rural areas might be interested in how Congress votes on agricultural bills. Voters living on the coast are probably interested in bills about controlling floods.

Candidates running for Congress try to convince the people of their state to vote for them.

Keeping People Safe

Members of Congress know safety is important to everyone. Federal laws protect people in every part of daily life. Labels must warn us if cleaning products are poisonous. Labels must list food ingredients. And drinking water must be tested for dangerous chemicals. Congress has also passed laws to limit pollution in the air we breathe.

Because of laws passed by Congress, packaged foods must contain labels that list the ingredients.

IF A PRODUCT MIGHT BE DANGEROUS FOR CHILDREN, FEDERAL LAW SAYS THAT IT MUST CONTAIN A WARNING LABEL.

▼

People especially want children to be safe. Congress does too. Federal laws require all products for children to be tested for safety. Schools must provide healthful meals to children. Congress has also passed laws to protect the privacy of internet users under thirteen years old.

In democratic countries such as the United States, the citizens get to elect new lawmakers every few years.

Vote for Change

If citizens are not happy with the work Congress has done, they can vote for new lawmakers. Citizens who are at least eighteen years old can vote for representatives every two years. Senators face elections every six years. Those under eighteen can make a difference too. If you have an idea that could make people's lives safer or easier, write to your congressperson. Remember, the legislative branch represents you!

Government Affects You

If you lived a century ago, you might be working in a factory for up to eighteen hours a day. Instead of doing schoolwork, children often ran dangerous equipment and carried heavy loads. By 1900, half of the states had passed laws that made child labor illegal. But Congress had to step in to pass a federal law that prevents children under the age of fourteen from working at most jobs.

Until 1938, it was legal for children of any age to work outside the home. Some performed dangerous work in factories and mills.

Who's Right?

Should Congress pass a law to ban restaurants from serving sugary drinks to children? People have strong opinions on this issue. Some people believe that laws must protect children's health. Children can suffer from tooth decay and other health problems from drinking too much soda or flavored milk. Other people believe that only parents can teach children to make healthful choices. They believe that a ban takes away a family's freedom to make its own rules.

What do you think? Should Congress decide what children can and cannot drink?

Glossary

chamber: a room or a division of a legislative body

committee: a group of people chosen to discuss a particular issue and make decisions or take action for a larger group

debate: a discussion in which people express different opinions

democracy: a form of government in which the people choose their leaders in elections

executive branch: the branch of government that carries out the laws of the United States or any state

federal: relating to the laws made and enforced by the central or national government

gavel: a small wooden hammer that is used to signal the beginning of a meeting or to call for quiet

judicial branch: the branch of government that interprets and applies laws and decides if they follow the Constitution

legislature: a group of people who have the power to make or change laws for a country or state

veto: to stop a bill from becoming a law

Learn More about the Legislative Branch

Books

Connors, Kathleen M. *How Does a Bill Become a Law?* New York: Gareth Stevens Publishing, 2018. This book introduces readers to the three branches of government and traces the steps a bill takes to become a law.

Cummings, Matthew. *What Is the Legislative Branch?* New York: Rosen Publishing, 2016. Explore the role the legislative branch plays in the federal and state government and meet some of the men and women who have worked there.

Krasner, Barbara. *Exploring the Executive Branch.* Minneapolis: Lerner Publications, 2020. Learn more about another branch of the US government.

Websites

Ben's Guide: The Legislative Branch
https://bensguide.gpo.gov/a-legislative
This interactive website allows students to explore each branch of government through colorful charts and games.

Brainpop: Branches of Goverment
https://www.brainpop.com/socialstudies/elections/branchesofgovernment/
From coding to making maps, this site gives students many ways to learn about the legislative branch.

Kids in the House
https://kids-clerk.house.gov/grade-school/
This site offers fascinating details about the roles of everyone in Congress.

Index

Photo Acknowledgments

Image credits: AP Photo/Carolyn Kaster, p. 4; Chip Somodevilla/Getty Images, pp. 5, 17, 20; Library of Congress (LC-DIG-pga-01711), p. 6; Alan Crosthwaite/Alamy Stock Photo, p. 7; DON EMMERT/AFP/Getty Images, p. 8; Architect of the Capitol, p. 9; Photo12/UIG/Getty Images, p. 10; Wikimedia Commons (public domain), p. 11; Xinhua News Agency/Getty Images, p. 12; Office of the Speaker of the House/Wikimedia Commons, p. 13; Jim Lo Scalzo/EPA/Anadolu Agency/Getty Images, p. 14; Archive Photos/Getty Images, p. 15; Joe Ravi/Shutterstock.com, p. 16; Collection of the U.S. House of Representatives, p. 18; Bettmann/Getty Images, p. 19; Library of Congress (LC-DIG-ppmsca-03196), p. 21; MANDEL NGAN/AFP/Getty Images, p. 22; Bettmann/Getty Images, p. 23; KEREM YUCEL/AFP/Getty Images, p. 24; Todd Strand/Independent Picture Service, p. 25; Jovan Nikolic/Shutterstock.com, p. 26; David Leaming/Portland Press Herald/Getty Images, p. 27; Library of Congress (LC-DIG-nclc-01127), p. 28; Brent Hofacker/Shutterstock.com, p. 29.

Cover: Tom Williams/CQ Roll Call/Getty Images.